My Bilingual Talking Dictionary

Japanese & English

First published in 2005 by Mantra Lingua
Global House, 303 Ballards Lane, London N12 8NP
www.mantralingua.com

This TalkingPEN edition 2009
Text copyright © 2005 Mantra Lingua
Illustrations copyright © 2005 Mantra Lingua
(except pages 4-9, 42-49 Illustrations copyright © 2005 Priscilla Lamont)
Audio copyright © 2009 Mantra Lingua

With thanks to the illustrators:
David Anstey, Dixie Bedford-Stockwell, Louise Daykin,
Alison Hopkins, Richard Johnson, Allan Jones,
Priscilla Lamont, Yokococo

All rights reserved

A CIP record for this book is available from the British Library

Hear each page of this talking book narrated with the RecorderPEN!
1) To get started touch the arrow button below with the RecorderPEN.
2) To hear the word in English touch the 'E' button at the top of the pages.
3) To hear the word spoken in an English sentence touch the 'S' button at the top of the pages.
4) To hear the language of your choice touch the 'L' button on the top of the pages.
5) Touch the square button below to hear more information about using the Dictionary with the RecorderPEN.

Start   Information

Contents　　もくじ

わたし Myself　page 4-5	うんそう Transport　page 26-27	うちゅう Space　page 50-51
ふく Clothes　page 6-7	かちく Farm Animals　page 28-29	てんき Weather　page 52-53
かぞく Family　page 8	やせいどうぶつ Wild Animals　page 30-31	じゅうにかげつ Months of the Year　page 54
うち Home　page 9	かいがん Seaside　page 32-33	きせつ Seasons　page 54
いえとかぐるい House and Contents　page 10-11	うんどうじょう Playground　page 34-35	ようび Days of the Week　page 55
くだもの Fruit　page 12-13	きょうしつ Classroom　page 36-37	とけい Telling the Time　page 55
やさい Vegetables　page 14-15	かばん School Bag　page 38-39	いろ Colours　page 56
たべものとのみもの Food and Drink　page 16-17	コンピューター Computers　page 40-41	かたち Shapes　page 56
しょくじのじかん Meal Time　page 18-19	ままごと Dressing Up　page 42-43	かず 1-20 Numbers 1-20　page 57
まち Town　page 20-21	おもちゃとゲーム Toys and Games　page 44-45	たいぎご Opposites　page 58-59
しょうてんがい High Street　page 22-23	スポーツ Sport　page 46-47	
こうつうあんぜん Road Safety　page 24-25	おんがく Music　page 48-49	さくいん Index　page 60-64

Myself

め
eyes

かみのけ
hair

くち
mouth

みみ
ears

は
teeth

て
hand

おやゆび
thumb

てくび
wrist

ゆび
fingers

どう
waist

あし
feet

あしゆび
toes

しあわせ
happy

かなしい
sad

おこる
angry

ねたむ
jealous

こうふん
excited

わたし

かお face
あたま head
はな nose
くび neck
うで arm
かた shoulders
おなか stomach
ひじ elbow
ひざ knee
せなか back
あしくび ankle
あし leg

きぶんがわるい sick

おなかがすいた hungry

こわがる scared

はにかむ shy

つかれた tired

5

Clothes

 コート coat

 スカーフ scarf

 ティーシャツ t-shirt

 ドレス dress

 スカート skirt

 カーディガン cardigan

 みずぎ swimming costume

 タイツ tights

 パンツ knickers

 くつ shoes

ふく

てぶくろ
gloves

ぼうし
hat

シャツ
shirt

セーター
jumper

ズボン
trousers

たんぱん
shorts

すいえいパンツ
swimming
trunks

トレーナー
trainers

くつした
socks

パンツ
underpants

Family

かぞく

Home うち

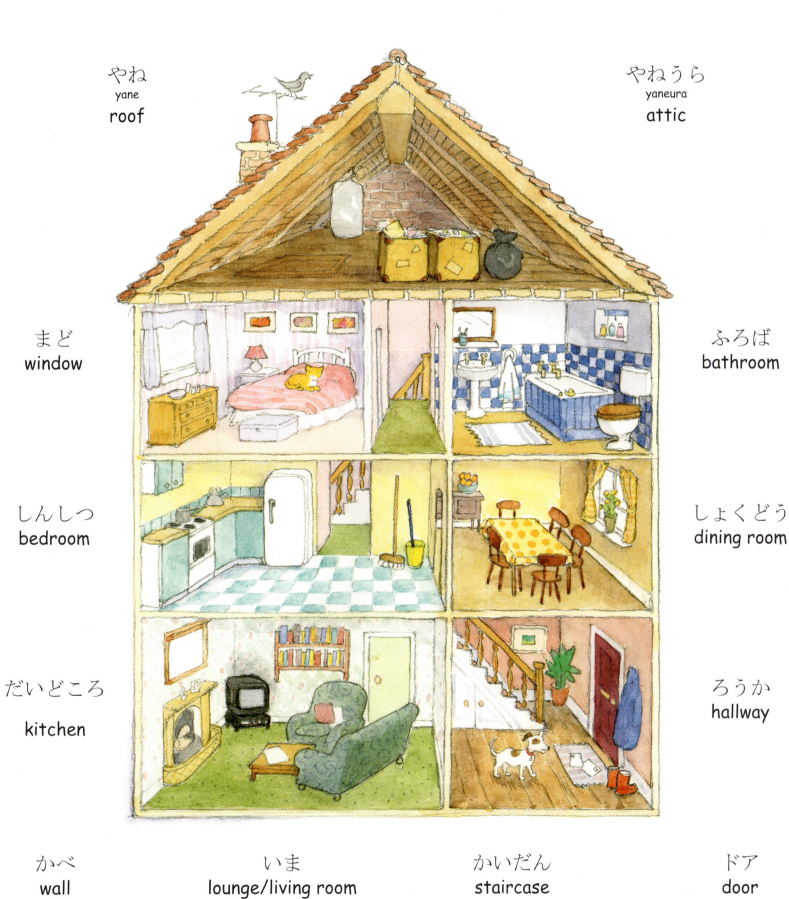

やね yane roof

やねうら yaneura attic

まど window

ふろば bathroom

しんしつ bedroom

しょくどう dining room

だいどころ kitchen

ろうか hallway

かべ wall

いま lounge/living room

かいだん staircase

ドア door

House and Contents

まくら
pillow

ベッド
bed

もうふ
blanket

ごみばこ
bin

せんぷうき
fan

ランプ
lamp

でんわ
telephone

せんたくき
washing machine

トースター
toaster

やかん
kettle

じゃぐち
tap

れいぞうこ
fridge

ガスだい
cooker

ながし
sink

いえとかぐるい

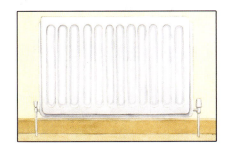
だんぼう
radiator

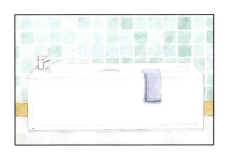
ふろ
bath

タオル
towel

かがみ
mirror

トイレ
toilet

トイレロール
toilet roll

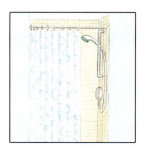
シャワー
shower

テレビ
television

ラジオ
radio

カーテン
curtains

とだな
cupboard

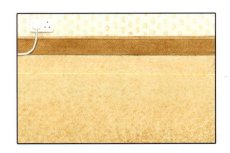
じゅうたん
carpet

ソファー
sofa

テーブル
table

Fruit

バナナ
banana

パパイヤ
papaya

なし
pear

メロン
melon

せいようすもも
plum

レモン
lemon

さくらんぼ
cherries

いちご
strawberries

くだもの

ぶどう
grapes

パイナップル
pineapple

マンゴー
mango

オレンジ
orange

もも
peach

りんご
apple

ライチー
lychees

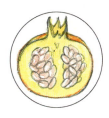
ざくろ
pomegranate

Vegetables

たまねぎ
onion

カリフラワー
cauliflower

じゃがいも
potato

とうもろこし
sweetcorn

きのこ
mushroom

トマト
tomato

まめ
beans

だいこん
radish

やさい

にんにく
garlic

かぼちゃ
pumpkin/squash

きゅうり
cucumber

ブロッコリー
broccoli

ピーマン
pepper/capsicum

にんじん
carrot

レタス
lettuce

グリーンピース
peas

Food and Drink

 パン bread

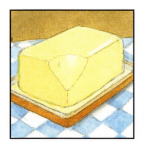 バター butter

 ジャム jam

 サンドイッチ sandwich

 さとう sugar

 はちみつ honey

 シリアル cereal

 ぎゅうにゅう milk

 めん noodles

 こめ/ごはん rice

 スパゲッティ spaghetti

 ピザ pizza

 にく meat

 さかな fish

 たまご egg

 チーズ cheese

たべものとのみもの

チョコレート
chocolate

おかし
sweets

ケーキ
cake

デザート
pudding

ヨーグルト
yoghurt

アイスクリーム
ice cream

ビスケット
biscuit

ポテトチップス
crisps

ポテトフライ
chips

トマトケチャップ
ketchup

からし
mustard

スープ
soup

かじゅう
fruit juice

ミネラルウォーター
mineral water

しお
salt

こしょう
pepper

Meal Time

ナイフ
knife

フォーク
fork

さじ
spoon

はし
chopsticks

マグ
mug

カップ
cup

コップ
glass

18

しょくじのじかん

さら
plate

どんぶり
bowl

なべ
saucepan

ちゅうかなべ
wok

フライパン
frying pan

まほうびん
flask

べんとうばこ
lunchbox

Town

スーパー
supermarket

ちゅうしゃじょう
car park

スポーツセンター
sports centre

としょかん
library

けいさつしょ
police station

えき
train station

しょうぼうしょ
fire station

まち

びょういん
hospital

こうえん
park

えいがかん
cinema

しゅうりこうじょう
garage

バスステーション
bus station

みせ
shops/stores

がっこう
school

High Street

レストラン
restaurant

はなや
florist

ばいてん
newspaper stand

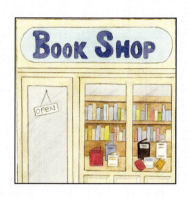

ほんや
book shop

にくや
butcher

ゆうびんきょく
post office

さかなや
fishmonger

しょうてんがい

やおや
greengrocer

くすりや
chemist

パンや
bakery

ぎんこう
bank

おもちゃや
toyshop

きっさてん
coffee shop

びようい ん
biyouin
hairdresser

Road Safety

どうろ
road

こうつうしんごう
traffic light

とまれ/あるくな
red man

すすめ/あるけ
green man

あかり
lights

はんしゃぶつ
reflector

ヘルメット
cycle helmet

おうだんほどう
pedestrian crossing

こうつうあんぜん

すすめ
go

とまれ
stop

みろ
look

きけ
listen

つうがくろ
children crossing

みどりのおばさん
school crossing
patrol officer

シートベルト
seat belt

ほどう
pavement

Transport

ひこうき
aeroplane

トラック
lorry/truck

じどうしゃ
car

バス
coach

ふね
boat

じてんしゃ
bicycle

でんしゃ
train

うんそう

オートバイ
motorbike

ヘリコプター
helicopter

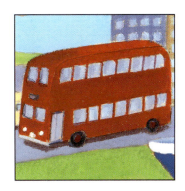
バス
bus

しでん
tram

トレーラー
caravan

ふね
ship

じんりきしゃ
rickshaw

Farm Animals

とり
bird

うま
horse

あひる
duck

ねこ
cat

やぎ
goat

うさぎ
rabbit

きつね
fox

かちく

うし
cow

いぬ
dog

ひつじ
sheep

ねずみ
mouse

めんどり
hen

ろば
donkey

がちょう
goose

Wild Animals

さる
monkey

ぞう
elephant

へび
snake

しまうま
zebra

ライオン
lion

かば
hippopotamus

いるか
dolphin

くじら
whale

やせいどうぶつ

パンダ
panda bear

きりん
giraffe

らくだ
camel

とら
tiger

くま
bear

ペンギン
penguin

わに
crocodile

さめ
shark

Seaside

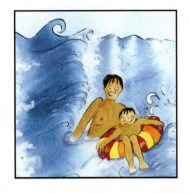
うみ
sea

なみ
waves

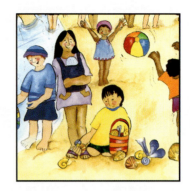
すなはま
beach

きゅうごいん
lifeguard

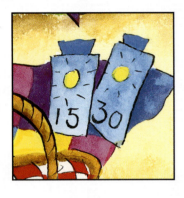
サンローション
sun lotion

かいがら
shells

こいし
pebbles

かいそう
seaweed

かいがん

かいすいのみずたまり
rock pool

かに
crab

ひとで
starfish

デッキチェア
deckchair

すな
sand

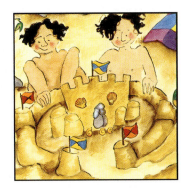
すなのしろ
sandcastle

バケツ
bucket

シャベル
spade

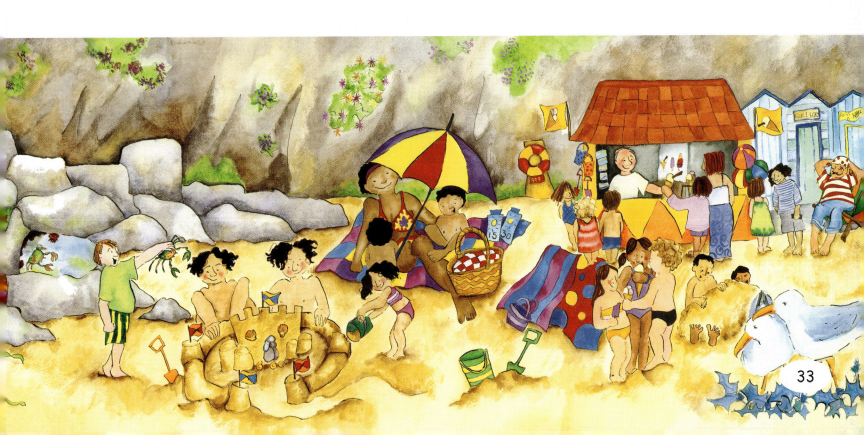

Playground

ぶらんこ
buranco
swing

かいてんもくば
kaitenmokuba
roundabout

シーソー
shiisou
seesaw

すなば
sunaba
sandpit

トンネル
tonneru
tunnel

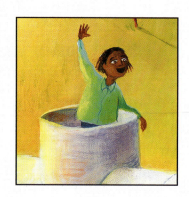

はいる
hairu
in

でる
deru
out

スキップ
sukkipu
skip

うんどうじょう

ジャングルジム
jangurujimu
climbing frame

うえ
ue
up

すべりだい
suberidai
slide

した
shita
down

のりこえる
norikoeru (climb over)
over

くぐる
kuguru (go through/under)
under

まえ
mae
in front

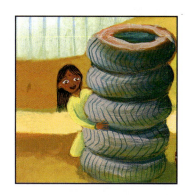
うしろ
ushiro
behind

35

The Classroom

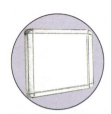
ホワイトボード
white board

こくばん
chalk board

つくえ
desk

いす
isu
chair

カレンダー
calendar

テープレコーダー
tape recorder

カセットテープ
cassette tape

けいさんき
calculator

きょうしつ

せんせい
teacher

ほん
books

かみ
paper

えのぐ
paint

えふで
paintbrush

はさみ
scissors

のり
glue

セロハンテープ
sticky tape

School Bag

ノート
nouto
writing book

さんすうのノート
sansou no nouto
maths book

フォルダー
folder

じょうぎ
ruler

ぶんどき
protractor

えんぴつ
pencil

えんぴつけずり
pencil sharpener

かばん

きょうかしょ
reading book

クレヨン
crayon

ひも
string

おかね
money

コンパス
compass

けしごむ
rubber/eraser

フェルトペン
felt tip pen

Computers

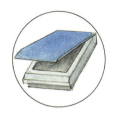
スキャナー
sukyanaa
scanner

コンピューター
kompyutaa
computer

モニター
monitor

キーボード
keyboard

マウス
mouse

マウスマット
mouse mat

コンピューター

プリンター
printer

がめん
screen

インターネット
internet

でんしメール
email

シーディー
cd disc

フロッピー
floppy disc

Dressing Up

うちゅうひこうし
astronaut

けいさつかん
police person

じゅうい
vet

しょうぼうし
firefighter

げいじゅつか
artist

てんしゅ
shop keeper

きしゅ
jockey

カウボーイ
cowboy

コック
chef

ままごと

かんごふ
nurse

きかいこう
mechanic

うんてんし
train driver

バレリーナ
ballet dancer

アイドル
pop star

ピエロ
clown

かいぞく
pirate

まほうつかい
wizard

いしゃ
doctor

Toys and Games

ふうせん
balloon

ビーズ
beads

ボードゲーム
board game

にんぎょう
doll

にんぎょうのいえ
doll's house

たこ
kite

パズル
puzzle

なわとびのなわ
skipping rope

こま
spinning top

おもちゃとゲーム

つみき
building blocks

チェス
chess

さいころ
dice

ビーだま
marbles

トランプ
playing cards

あやつりにんぎょう
puppet

ぬいぐるみのくま
teddy bear

おもちゃのでんしゃ
train set

おもちゃのくるま
toy car

Sport

バスケット
basketball

ボール
ball

クリケット
cricket

バドミントン
badminton

すいえい
swimming

ローラースケート
roller skates

ラケット
racquet

アイススケート
ice skates

スポーツ

テニス
tennis

バット
bat

ネットボール
netball

サッカー
football

サイクリング
cycling

ラグビー
rugby

スケートボード
skateboard

ホッケー
hockey

Music

 たいこ drum

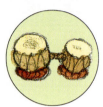 タブラ tabla

 クラリネット clarinet

 フルート flute

 ハープ harp

 キーボード keyboard

 ギター guitar

 ふめんだい music stand

おんがく

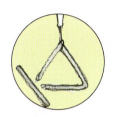
トライアングル
musical triangle

トランペット
trumpet

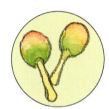
マラカス
maracas

ガンガン
gan gan

ピアノ
piano

リコーダー
recorder

バイオリン
violin

もっきん
xylophone

Space

 たいよう
sun

 すいせい
Mercury

 きんせい
Venus

 ちきゅう
Earth

 つき
moon

 うちゅうせん
spaceship

 ながれぼし
shooting star

 ロケット
rocket

うちゅう

かせい
Mars

もくせい
Jupiter

どせい
Saturn

てんおうせい
Uranus

ほうきぼし
comet

ほし
stars

かいおうせい
Neptune

めいおうせい
Pluto

Weather

はれ
sunny

にじ
rainbow

あめ
rainy

かみなり
thunder

いなずま
lightning

あらし
stormy

てんき

かぜがつよい
windy

きりがかった
foggy

ゆき
snowy

くもり
cloudy

あられ
hail

こおりのはる
icy

Months of the Year

じゅうにかげつ

 いちがつ January

 にがつ February

 さんがつ March

 しがつ April

 ごがつ May

 ろくがつ June

 しちがつ July

 はちがつ August

 くがつ September

 じゅうがつ October

 じゅういちがつ November

 じゅうにがつ December

Seasons

きせつ

はる Spring なつ Summer あき Autumn/Fall ふゆ Winter モンスーン Monsoon

Days of the Week　　　　　　　　　　　　ようび

げつようび
Monday

かようび
Tuesday

すいようび
Wednesday

もくようび
Thursday

きんようび
Friday

どようび
Saturday

にちようび
Sunday

Telling the Time　　　　　　　　　　　　とけい

 とけい clock

 ひるま day

 よる night

 あさ morning

 ゆうがた evening

 うでどけい watch

 じゅうごふんすぎ quarter past

 はん half past

 じゅうごふんまえ quarter to

Colours   いろ

あか　　　　　だいだいいろ　　　きいろ　　　　みどり
red　　　　　orange　　　　　yellow　　　　green

 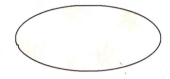 

くろ　　　　　しろ　　　　　はいいろ
black　　　　white　　　　grey

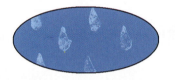  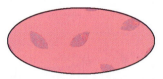 

あお　　　　　むらさき　　　ももいろ　　　ちゃいろ
blue　　　　　purple　　　　pink　　　　　brown

Shapes   かたち

   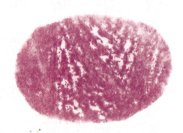

まる　　　　　ほし　　　　　さんかく　　　だえんけい
circle　　　　star　　　　　triangle　　　oval

 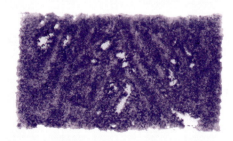 

えんすいけい　ちょうほうけい　しかく
cone　　　　　rectangle　　　square

Numbers 1-20   かず　１－２０

 1 いち　one   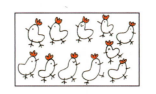 11 じゅういち　eleven

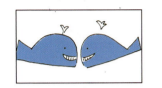 2 に　two    12 じゅうに　twelve

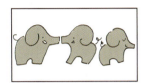 3 さん　three    13 じゅうさん　thirteen

 4 し　four   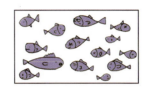 14 じゅうし　fourteen

 5 ご (go)　five    15 じゅうご　fifteen

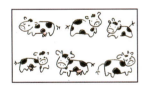 6 ろく　six    16 じゅうろく　sixteen

 7 しち　seven   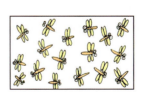 17 じゅうしち　seventeen

 8 はち　eight   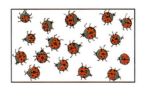 18 じゅうはち　eighteen

 9 きゅう　nine   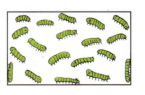 19 じゅうく　nineteen

 10 じゅう　ten    20 にじゅう　twenty

Opposites

はやい　　　おそい
fast　　　　slow

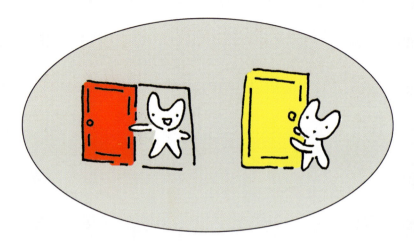

あいてる　　しまってる
open　　　　closed

おおきい　　ちいさい
large　　　　small

ぬれてる　　かわいてる
wet　　　　　dry

あつい　　さむい
hot　　　　cold

あまい　　すっぱい
sweet　　　sour

たいぎご

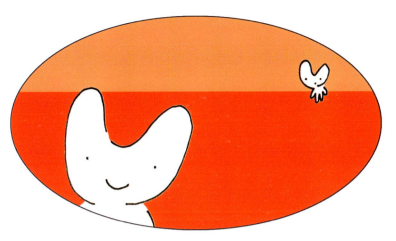

ちかい	とおい
near	far

ひだり	みぎ
left	right

まえ	うしろ
front	back

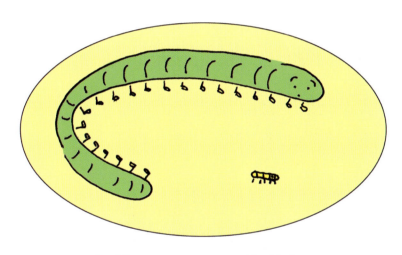

ながい	みじかい
long	short

おもい	かるい
heavy	light

から	まんぱい
empty	full

Index

Search for a word by picture or by the English word

Classroom Page 36-37	teacher	socks	pink	printer	car mechanic	**Family** Page 8
books	white board	swimming costume	purple	scanner	chef	aunt
calculator	**Clothes** Page 6-7	swimming trunks	red	screen	clown	baby
calendar	cardigan	t-shirt	white	**Days of the Week** Page 55	cowboy	brother
cassette/ tape	coat	tights	yellow	Monday	doctor	daughter
chair	dress	trainers	**Computers** Page 40-41	Tuesday	firefighter	father
chalk board	gloves	trousers	cd disc	Wednesday	jockey	 grandfather
desk	hat	underpants	computer	Thursday	nurse	 grandmother
glue	jumper	**Colours** Page 56	email	Friday	pirate	mother
paint	knickers	black	floppy disc	Saturday	police person	sister
 paintbrush	scarf	blue	internet	Sunday	pop star	son
paper	shirt	brown	keyboard	**Dressing Up** Page 42-43	shop keeper	uncle
scissors	shoes	green	monitor	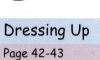 artist	train driver	**Farm Animals** Page 28-29
sticky tape	shorts	grey	mouse	astronaut	vet	bird
tape recorder	skirt	orange	mouse mat	ballet dancer	wizard	cat

Meal Time
Page 18-19

- bowl
- chopsticks
- cup
- flask
- fork
- frying pan
- glass
- knife
- lunchbox
- mug
- plate
- saucepan
- spoon
- wok

Months of the Year
Page 54

- January
- February
- March
- April
- May
- June
- July
- August
-  September
- October
- November
- December

Music
Page 48-49

- clarinet
- drum
- flute
- gan gan
- guitar
- harp
- keyboard
- maracas
- musical triangle
- music stand
- piano
- recorder
- tabla
- trumpet
- violin
- xylophone

Myself
Page 4-5

- angry
- ankle
- arm
- back
- ears
- elbow
- excited
- eyes
- face
- feet
- fingers
- hair
- hand
- happy
- head
- hungry
- jealous
- knee
- leg
- mouth
- neck
- nose
- sad
- scared
- shoulders
- shy
- sick
- stomach
- teeth
- thumb
- tired
- toes
- waist
- wrist

Numbers 1-20
Page 57

- one
- two
- three
- four
- five
- six
- seven
- eight
- nine
- ten
- eleven
- twelve
-  thirteen
- fourteen
- fifteen
- sixteen
- seventeen
- eighteen
- nineteen
- twenty

Opposites
Page 58-59

- back
- closed
- cold
- dry
- empty
- far
- fast
- front
- full
- heavy
- hot
- large
- left
- light
- long
- near

rugby	cinema	chess	boat	cucumber	foggy	crocodile
skateboard	fire station	dice	bus	garlic	hail	dolphin
swimming	garage	doll	car	lettuce	icy	elephant
tennis	hospital	doll's house	caravan	mushroom	lightning	giraffe

Telling the Time Page 55

	library	kite	coach	onion	rainbow	hippopotamus
clock	park	marbles	helicopter	peas	rainy	lion
day	police station	playing cards	lorry/truck	pepper/capsicum	snowy	 monkey
 evening	school	puppet	motorbike	potato	stormy	panda bear
half past	shops/stores	 puzzle	rickshaw	pumpkin/squash	sunny	penguin
morning	 sports centre	skipping rope	ship	radish	thunder	shark
night	supermarket	spinning top	train	sweetcorn	windy	snake
quarter past	train station	teddy bear	tram	tomato	**Wild Animals** Page 30-31	tiger
quarter to	**Toys and Games** Page 44-45	train set	**Vegetables** Page 14-15	**Weather** Page 52-53	bear	whale
watch	balloon	toy car	beans	cloudy	camel	zebra

Town Page 20-21

	beads	**Transport** Page 26-27	broccoli	
bus station	board game	aeroplane	carrot	
car park	building blocks	bicycle	cauliflower	